JOLANDA

I PRAY THAT YOU CONTINUE TO GROW
IN THE KNOWLEDGE OF THE RIGHTS
YOU HAVE IN CHRIST THAT CAME
BY HIS BLOOD.

CONGRATULATIONS ON YOUR ACHIEVEMENTS

LOVE YOU

UNCLE SAM

YOUR BLOOD BOUGHT RIGHTS

UNVEILING THE SIMPLICITY OF COVENANT FOR THE PURPOSES OF KINGDOM ACTIVITY

SAM MASAMBA SR.

Your Blood Bought Rights: Unveiling The Simplicity Of Covenant For The Purposes of Kingdom Activity

ISBN: 9798663969642
Printed in the United Kingdom
© 2020 by SAM MASAMBA SR.

Published by Four Stones Publishing, The TAD Centre, Ormesby Road, Middlesbrough TS3 7SF
Cover Design by Hampton & Shaw

VISIT OUR OFFICIAL WEBSITE: SamMasamba.com

Most Word studies come from Strong's Exhaustive Concordance of the Bible by James Strong (Care of Hendrickson Publishers). Most definitions come from Merriam–Webster Dictionary online.

DEDICATION

I dedicate this book to my Father Apostle Ralph Masamba who has been a great inspiration in my life. And to the woman who was the foundation of my walk and belief in Christ, who dedicated her whole life till her passing on to the preaching of the Gospel leaving an impact on thousands in this generation, Elizabeth Masamba, My Mum. This book is to celebrate your legacy that still lives on. You are forever loved and missed.

Also, to my Pastors and spiritual parents Apostles Tony and Cynthia Brazelton and the many men and women of God who have directly transformed my life through the preaching of the Word of faith. I celebrate you and am forever grateful.

ABOUT THE AUTHOR

Sam Masamba Sr. is a spiritual leader, leadership coach, campus pastor, keynote speaker and author. He leads a diverse, ever-growing and vibrant church within the United Kingdom and leads a social initiative called MenCave, a community-based enterprise that educates, equips & empowers marginalised men in society. He is also the founder and president of Four Stones Consultancy, a forward-thinking ministry and leadership consultancy firm that helps pastors, leaders and pioneers grow in spiritual wisdom, marketplace effectiveness and ministerial productivity.

ALSO BY SAM MASAMBA SR.

The Davidic Church

Pursuing Holiness

The Spirit of Faith

Realms of Authority

The New Believer's Guide

YOUR BLOOD BOUGHT RIGHTS

CONTENTS

FOREWORD

God has given many promises and blessings in the Word that we are not all aware of; many are also not aware that the blessings and promises are, in fact, the finished work of the Cross of Jesus Christ. 2nd Peter 1:3 states that "everything we could ever need for life and godliness has already been deposited in us by his divine power."

That power is in the Blood of Jesus. And if you are a citizen of the Kingdom of God, you have a <u>blood bought right</u> to the promises of God. We no longer need to labour or perform to get God to do anything; it's already done! The only thing left for us to do now is to believe and receive what He has done for us. Philemon 1:6 states "that the communication of thy faith may become effectual by the acknowledging of every good thing which is in you in Christ Jesus."

When God reveals to you what Jesus has already purchased for you, it's time to acknowledge what is in you in Christ Jesus. Pastor Sam does a masterful job in bringing clarity to the different covenants God made with man. God has chosen to relate to man, or have a relationship with man on the basis of a covenant agreement. Knowing and understanding that Christ brought a new covenant agreement from God to man, is the difference between having the blessings God promised, and not having what God promised at all. Getting this right has huge ramifications.

In this book by Pastor Sam Masamba "Your Blood Bought Rights", he will help you to navigate and take possession of the life that God has provided for you through His covenant agreement. I firmly believe that you, your relationship with God, your walk, your faith, and your understanding will be enlightened by this book. You will discover that your healing, deliverance, prosperity, victory has already been purchased through the precious blood of Jesus and by the grace of God.

Apostle Tony Brazelton
Founder, Victory Christian Ministries International (VCMI)

.

INTRODUCTION

'Every person with no understanding of the Covenant
will walk focusing on what they can't do instead of what
they can do'.

It was 2004 and my church mission team and I
embarked on a mission trip to the Republic of Ireland.
Most of us grew up in a landlocked country in Africa,
and had never had the wonderful opportunity of
travelling anywhere by sea. As we took our first steps
onto the huge ship, a chill slithered down my spine.
We had been waiting for months, though it felt like
decades, and we were finally boarding the cruise ship.
We walked around to check the ship out for a few
hours, quite excited with it being our first time.
Coming from England (Birkenhead Port) going to
Dublin, Ireland, meant that the trip would be an
overnight one and that at some point we would need to
eat.

By 7pm we were more than ready for supper. We walked to the other end of the ship and got on the elevator and headed up to the Ralph Deck, which was on the third floor of the ship. We were surprised when they handed us the menus. There was a choice of salmon, chicken parmesan, lobster, crab and we were told we could eat whatever we want and as much of it as we wanted. The desserts looked even better, I could already notice my favourites: apple pie and chocolate cake. The only thing that the waiter forgot to mention was the price of the food. To make matters worse, the menus didn't have prices either.

In the dining hall, there was a buffet dinner setup and it seemed some people (that looked like VIPs in our site) had access to this food without limitations. None of us amongst my team knew how much the food was and by the way that the food was laid out, we could only assume that these people had paid a huge amount for them to get access to the meal. So because of our ignorance we gazed longingly into the dining room and watch the people eat the food while we stood on the outside watching.

After some considerable amount of time, I decided, due to the increasing levels of hunger, I wanted to ask one of the waiters how much a portion of fries was? I didn't want to spend too much so I assumed a portion of fries will be sufficient, for that moment in time. What I was told shaped the theme of this entire book.

Those enticing, beautifully prepared and almost perfect meals were included in our ticket fare. Even though it was a huge relief to the team and I, we couldn't help but regret the hour and a half that we had wasted only because we were ignorant of what rightly belonged to us. Because of a lack of knowledge we could not access something we had already purchased. By the time we went for the meal, most of the dishes had already finished and we just had to eat what was now the unwanted leftovers. What a shame! If only we knew.

How many Christian people are living in a place of ignorance when God, through the precious blood of his Son, has already bought your rights?

When it comes to living a breakthrough reality it will come only through understanding the Covenant that

God made with Jesus Christ on our behalf. A person with no understanding of the Covenant will consistently walk focusing on what they cannot do instead of realising and accepting what they can do. Understanding your Covenant Right lifts your expectation and opens channels for you to freely receive what is already yours.

In this book, I will disclose exactly how the Blood of Jesus has already accomplished all we need pertaining to a life of peace, joy, and godliness. By dividing the Word of truth, we will finally understand what Jesus Christ has truly done for us and how we can all enter into the dinning room of His grace and eat the abundance of His love that has been freely given.

"He died for it so that you don't have to die from it"

DIVIDING THE WORD OF TRUTH

'He died for it so that you don't have to die from it'

Before we begin, I want to lay some form of foundation so that we understand the premise of this teaching.

The Law of Moses includes the ten commandments and over six hundred laws that supports it. As valuable as they seemed at the time, the truth is, the Law represented elements of a system that led to our inevitable earthly and spiritual death, and did not give us any pathway to eternal life through Jesus Christ.

When Moses arrived with the Ten Commandments for the people of Israel, he saw that they had sinned (broken the Law) and he reacted angrily, breaking the tablets and ordering the death of three thousand people (read Exodus 32:28). In Acts 2, as the Holy Ghost came to the Earth, the result was three thousand people receiving Christ and becoming saved. What was lost by failing to adhere to the Law, the Kingdom of Heaven has gained and recovered thousands of years later through the Grace of God. What was lost in law was recovered by grace. This book is grounded on this truth.

The Law of Moses operates on a system of conditional blessings. The Law places a demand for performance, while grace is a constant supply of help. The Law requires energy, effort and human strength while grace empowers, strengthens, and supports us, our daily growth. We must stay abreast of the facts of Scriptures. In order for you to effectively draw from and enjoy the high priestly ministry of Jesus today, you must understand the New Testament, of which Jesus is the High Priest and Mediator.

When most people read the Bible, they read it from an old-covenant perspective. This way of reading Scripture often puts our focus on sin, condemnation, and self-effort, mainly because of the emphasis of Moses' Law. The Old Testament has valuable lessons to teach us, but we no longer need to live under the old covenant and the Law of Moses. The current covenant of grace was established after Jesus died on the cross and was raised from the dead, and it provides for us a reality of freedom that was nonexistent under the law. If we struggle (or refuse) to read our Bibles through the lens of the undeserved favour and merciful love of God towards us, we will never truly understand how the finished works of Jesus has the power to impact our lives in every single way.

Your breakthrough doesn't respond to your prayer but rather, it is accelerated by your understanding of the unbreakable covenant you have with your Father in Heaven. When we talk about covenant, it is a concept that involves reforming and conforming to a brand new identity and reality. You are no longer conformed to your social status, your age, colour, gender, race, or education, but you have assumed a new identity in Christ.

The way you see yourself will determine where you go and what you get. God's grace over your life is unlimited, of course, that is without question. But the truth of the matter is it the degree at which it functions and works for you, is closely tied to the degree of vision that you have about yourself. Just like God told Abraham, He is saying the same to you: as far as your eyes can see, I will give it to you.

2 Timothy 2:15

Do your best to be the kind of person God will accept and give yourself to him. Be a worker who has no reason to be ashamed of his work, one who applies the true teaching in the right way.

Paul instructs Timothy to rightly divide the word of truth, indicating to us all that the Bible is not as plain as it seems. If one does not properly understand the power of the Cross, it means they cannot rightly divide the word of truth.

How we understand Scripture profoundly impacts how we live our lives, and the results we experience. The Word can be divided correctly or incorrectly. The wrong interpretation of the Bible can lead us to the wrong conclusion.

Correctly dividing and analysing the Word of God empowers us to break free from negative emotions, destructive habits, or anything else weighing us down in our spirits. Conversely, incorrectly dividing it actually hinders us from experiencing God's best. Before the Cross, God's blessing depended on man's self-efforts and obedience, first. After the Cross, the requirements to be blessed changed from what we must do to believing in what Christ already did.

What this means for us is that any curse that was in effect before the cross has now been lifted, and we no longer have to fear it. The blessings have already been made available to us, and we receive them by faith. Jesus' blood neutralised any curse spoken over us, and we can speak the Word into any situation that opposes us. No one can curse what God has blessed.

God knew we were too weak to keep all the requirements of the law, which is why He abolished them by sending us Jesus. His grace is sufficient, and we can be grateful that He has replaced the need for our own works. Believing this changes our whole perspective. We can read the Bible all we want, but if we do not understand the true meaning of what God is trying to convey to us, we might as well be reading a fairy tale. Paul told Timothy:

2 Timothy 3:14-16

But you should continue following the teaching you learned. You know it is true because you know you can trust those who taught you. You have known the Holy Scriptures since you were a child. These Scriptures are able to make you wise. And that wisdom leads to salvation through faith in Christ Jesus. All Scripture is given by God. And all Scripture is useful for teaching and for showing people what is wrong in their lives. It is useful for correcting faults and teaching the right way to live.

The Bible tells us that the Holy Scriptures are profitable for Doctrine (which is learning) for Reprove (which is evidence), Corrections, Instructions, in righteousness, that the Man of God may be perfect, mature, and developed. The old Covenant, based on the Law, required that we first follow the letter of the Law in order to be blessed. Under the new Covenant, we now live under grace, because of what Jesus did when He shed His blood for us on the cross. As Believers, it is important for us to realise the difference.

The Bible is divided into two sections: pre-Cross (before the death of Jesus) and post-Cross (after the resurrection). The old covenant, or pre-Cross section, was based on works, and required that the children of Israel do something first in order to be blessed. Jesus shedding His blood on the Cross put us under the covenant of grace, the post-Cross section, which is based on His finished works. We do not have to "do" anything for God's blessing, we just have to accept and believe His promises. Operating as if we were still under the old, invalid covenant will not give us the results we want. God will never require from us anything He has not already put in us. He died for it, so that you don't have to die from it.

John 1:45

Philip found Nathanael and told him, "We have found the man that Moses wrote about in the law. The prophets wrote about him too. He is Jesus, the son of Joseph. He is from Nazareth."

25

The message of the prophets and of Moses was an attempt at revealing Christ. You will never know who you are until you know who He is, because the Revelation of who you are, is tied up in Him. "AS HE IS SO ARE YOU IN THIS WORLD".

1 John 4:17 (b)

because as He is, so are we in this world.

Jesus mediates only the New Testament,

Hebrews 8:6

"But now He has obtained a more excellent ministry, inasmuch as He is also Mediator of a better covenant, which was established on better promises"

Saints, in order for us to be fully equipped Kingdom Participants, we have to understand that the New Testament is not a compliment but a replacement.

Galatians 1:6

"A short time ago God chose you to follow him. He chose you through his grace that came through Christ. But now

I am amazed that you are already turning away and believing something different from the Good News we told you".

You cannot be saved by grace and at the same time, live by works. Not only is it contradictory, it is illogical as well! In His desire to teach them, Jesus wanted his disciples to have the ability first to receive what He really wanted to say. What we need to take note of is that the disciples Jesus was talking to were still not convinced and they struggled to understand the Word from His perspective. They were a people under an Old Covenant mentality, simply because that's all they had known. This explains why He spoke in parables, as they were low-minded in spirit, unable to comprehend the real issues that would point the truth of the Word back to Himself. So, in John 16, He wants the Spirit of truth to first boost their receiving capacity so that they can comprehend the truth.

John 16:12-13

"I have so much more to tell you, but it is too much for you to accept now. But when the Spirit of truth comes, he will lead you into all truth. He will not speak his own words.

He will speak only what he hears and will tell you what will happen in the future.

The message of the Bible or Church is not houses, church buildings, cars, possessions or even the Holy Ghost but it is JESUS, for the Holy Spirit will not speak of Himself, but rather His purpose is to reveal Christ. Even though we benefit from all these things, the emphasis is on Jesus' death, burial and resurrection and the abundant authoritative and purpose-driven life in the Kingdom that He came to deliver to us.

So, the message that Jesus taught in the Gospels was focusing on challenging the mindset in a setting that was religious and law bound. It was a message that was supposed to bring non-believers to faith. Therefore, the message of the church is the Epistles because that is what the Holy Spirit spoke through Apostle Paul. In the letters or epistles that Paul wrote, we find an understanding of where our position in Christ lies and the authority we have through the finished work of the Cross. That's why Paul says 'You need a revelation that the eyes of your understanding be enlightened'.

Ephesians 1:18

"I pray that God will open your minds to see his truth. Then you will know the hope that he has chosen us to have. You will know that the blessings God has promised his holy people are rich and glorious"

The ministry of the New Testament is the foundation behind the ministry of revelatory truth. It is because of the writings of Paul that we are able to fully comprehend the power that lies behind the revealed Word of Grace.

You must acknowledge that the Doctrinal books starts from Romans since Acts is a narrative book. The Doctrine we believe is unapologetically the Doctrine of Christ which is the message of Grace.

Acts 20:2

"Now I am putting you in God's care. I am depending on the message about his grace to make you strong. That message is able to give you the blessings that God gives to all his holy people."

The church can never be built until the message of Grace is preached, and preached effectively. When the Old Testament is preached it always find faults. Much emphasis is put on the wrong they did, and the attachment of sin.

If you notice, it is a fault-finding testament. We read about Samson and Delilah, Rehab the Harlot, David and Bathsheba, Abraham, and the Maid and men and women highly flawed and with many faults, but in the New Testament faults are not recorded. In fact, they are openly forgiven and forgotten. In the Old Testament, faults and flaws were exposed with immediate judgement and punishment due to the Law, while flaws and weaknesses are blotted out and forgiven through the Grace of Jesus in the New Testament we live in and enjoy today.

Hebrews 11:1-2

Now faith is the substance of things hoped for, the evidence of things not seen. For by it the Elders obtained a good testimony...

Take notice how the New Testament sees all these names mentioned before as Elders who obtained good reports. The Testament of Grace is not fault-finding but it is a testament of a relationship of a Father and Son, and a good father does not find fault. Love (and the grace is birthed by that love) always covers a multitude of sin (see 1 Peter 4:8)

Hebrews 8:10-12

"This is the new agreement I will give the people of Israel. I will give this agreement in the future, says the Lord: I will put my laws in their minds, and I will write my laws on their hearts. I will be their God, and they will be my people, None of them shall teach his neighbour, and none his brother, saying, 'Know the Lord,' for all shall know Me, from the least of them to the greatest of them. For I will be merciful to their unrighteousness, and their sins and their lawless deeds I will remember no more."

That is why when you receive Jesus, you repent from your sins and you confess HIM (not sin) as Lord, then what He accomplished for you takes care of your faults.

31

Romans 8:6-9

For to be carnally minded is death, but to be spiritually minded is life and peace. Because the carnal mind is enmity against God; for it is not subject to the law of God, nor indeed can be. So then, those who are in the flesh cannot please God. But you are not in the flesh but in the Spirit, if indeed the Spirit of God dwells in you. Now if anyone does not have the Spirit of Christ, he is not His.

Once you are born again, you are not in the flesh but in the Spirit. In the Old Testament were conditions but in the New Testament there are no conditions. In the New Testament, all the believer has to do is to know that they have an identity in Christ. The Old Testament justified no-one, and this is simply because the Word tells us that:

Romans 3:20

"...no one can be made right with God by following the law. The law only shows us our sin".

His Blood and His Grace justifies us.

Romans 5:1

We have been made right with God because of our faith. So, we have peace with God through our Lord Jesus Christ.

In the New Testament, Grace teaches us,

Galatians 3:10-12

For as many as are of the works of the law are under the curse; for it is written, "Cursed is everyone who does not continue in all things which are written in the book of the law, to do them."But that no one is justified by the law in the sight of God is evident, for "the just shall live by faith. "Yet the law is not of faith, but "the man who does them shall live by them."

In this new reality of grace, we are commissioned to live a life powered by faith. Our righteousness comes by faith. Our acceptance of His love comes by faith. Our authority in Christ comes by faith. Our dominion and influence over our world comes by faith. Our Word tells us that Christ has redeemed from the curse of the law.

The promise of the Spirit can only be received through faith, but in order to do so, we need a better understanding of this promise.

Let us look into the power of the covenant promise that was made not only to Abraham, but to his Seed, Christ Jesus. Understanding this allows us to understand exactly where we stand, what we have ownership of and what we are to do with this abundance of fulfilled promises.

'The New Testament (covenant) is unconditional and is life everlasting'

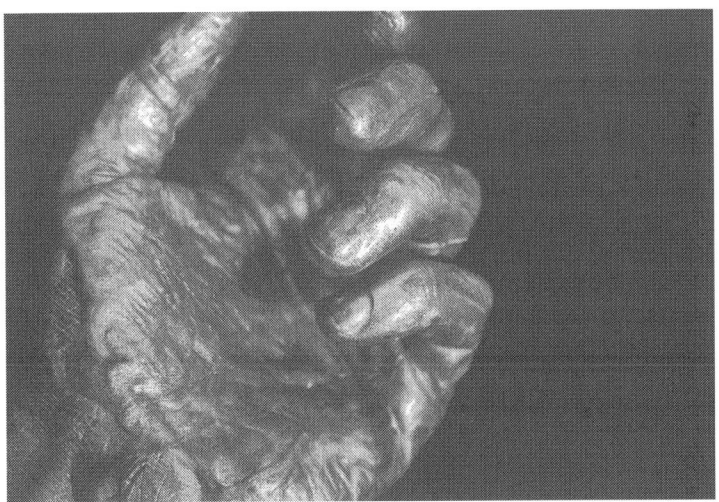

UNDERSTANDING COVENANTS

'The New Testament (covenant) is unconditional and is life everlasting'

It is very vital for every believer to understand that the Blood of Jesus has brought us into a brand new covenant, which the Paul's letter to the Hebrews describes as the "better covenant than the one of the Old Testament".

When Paul uses the word better, he simply means that this covenant comes with a package containing better advantages and privileges. All of this makes up what we know to be "Good News" but to know exactly how much better they are, we must understand what the promises of the old covenant were in the first place. In Abraham's day, and frankly even still up to today, a blood covenant signifies an absolute and unbreakable guarantee of a man's word. Nothing short of a blood agreement could have convinced Abraham of God's desire to bless him. By cutting the covenant with him, God communicated His unfailing love and fidelity on a level and with a symbol of promise Abraham could easily relate to and understand. God was establishing a love relationship with him that could not be broken without the penalty of death.

In order to see just how that old covenant compares to the new one we have with the Father today, we need to see what the covenant God cut with Abraham involved. That way we can begin to see clearly why ours is even better.

Jeremiah 31:31-33

Behold, the days come, saith the Lord, that I will make a new covenant with the house of Israel, and with the house of Judah: Not according to the covenant that I made with their fathers in the day that I took them by the hand to bring them out of the land of Egypt; which my covenant they brake, although I was an husband unto them, saith the Lord: But this shall be the covenant that I will make with the house of Israel; After those days, saith

the Lord, I will put my law in their inward parts, and write it in their hearts; and will be their God, and they shall be my people.

For us to understand the New Covenant that Jesus brought, we must first understand what the word covenant means, how it is established and how it is attained!

In ancient times, for a covenant to be established there had to be blood. We see this when God made a covenant with Abraham in Genesis 17. Even so now because of the Blood of our precious Jesus we have been brought into a new and everlasting covenant.

Jeremiah 33:20-22

Thus saith the Lord; If ye can break my covenant of the day, and my covenant of the night, and that there should not be day and night in their season; Then may also my covenant be broken with David my servant, that he should not have a son to reign upon his throne; and with the Levites the priests, my ministers. As the host of heaven cannot be numbered, neither the sand of the sea meas-

ured: so will I multiply the seed of David my servant, and the Levites that minister unto me.

The word "covenant" is mentioned 316 times in about 95 verses and there are eight noteworthy "types" of covenants outlined throughout Scripture:

• The "Edenic" Covenant: Originating from the Garden of Eden, based on life and death, it was conditional (Genesis 1:26).

• The "Adamic" Covenant: A covenant of life after the fall of man (Genesis 3:14).

• The "Noahic" Covenant: A covenant promise or vow made by God to Noah never to destroy the Earth by water ever again (Genesis 9).

• The "Abrahamic" Covenant: This was a foundation and a prelude to the New Testament Covenant that was to come. God instituted the promise of blessing to Abraham that we are heirs will inherit at a later stage (Genesis 15).

- The "Mosaic" Covenant: This Covenant represents the wall of partition, which separated Jews and the Gentiles. This was represented by the curtain (veil) and was conditional (Exodus 24).

- The Covenant of the land

- The "Davidic" Covenant: It was unconditional and it has unending royal lineage. An Everlasting Kingdom from the House of David (2nd Samuel 7).

- The New Testament Covenant: The final, everlasting and unconditional Covenant of Grace.

In the book of Matthew, we see the lineage that connects Jesus to Abraham and David. God will always deal with you from this point of operation. David was an archetype rooted in Kingdom, while Abraham was a patriarch rooted in Covenant. God is both the initiator and the administrator of the Covenant which means He sets the terms and superintendents the execution of that Covenant in order to make sure that what was written in the Covenant go to the rightful owner.

There are two words in the bible that best describes the word Covenant:

The Hebrew word for covenant is Berit, which means Covenant, alliance, pledge, treaty, league, constitution or agreement. The Greek word for covenant is Diatheke means disposition, settlement carried out after the owner of a will dies, an arrangement, Testament, will.

The word "Berit" has the underlining message of cutting. Every covenant in the Bible always has a token of remembrance just as we see with the Rainbow in the covenant promise made to Noah, the instruction of circumcision given to Abraham and even our tradition of wearing wedding ring as a confirmation of holy matrimony. In the New Testament, as tokens of remembrance to symbolise the New Covenant in Christ, we have bread and wine.

The right Greek word in the New Testament for translating covenant here should have been "SUNTHEKE" not "DIATHEKE", but "SUNTHEKE" has the connotation of two equal parties coming together in the covenant. Whereas

41

"diatheke" has a connotation of the settlement by a predetermined will of the owner. Meaning that the superior one sets the terms and the other parts' position is either to decline or accept the terms.

In our Covenant with God, He sets terms and also administers the execution of the Covenant. The beauty of the New Covenant, however, is that God has with our Lord Jesus freely offered us the Kingdom benefits of prosperity, healing, peace, protection simply because Jesus has already paid the necessary price. When you accept Jesus Christ as your personal Lord and Saviour, and believe and receive the Covenant blessing that comes with it, you have no choice but to be healed, prosper, to be peaceful. The challenge is this is something you receive by faith through grace and not by your personal effort or works. As mentioned before, there are two types of Covenants: i) conditional and ii) unconditional. The Abrahamic Covenant made in Genesis 17 is the basis of the New Testament and the New Testament is nothing but a confirmation, a consummation in the blood of Jesus of the promises that God had already made to Abraham. It is an unconditional Covenant.

Ephesians 2:11

Wherefore remember, that ye being in time past Gentiles in the flesh, who are called Uncircumcision by that which is called the Circumcision in the flesh made by hands.

(Note: Gentiles was anybody who was not a Jew).

Gentiles are simply human beings without Christ. God desires all of humanity to be saved by the Blood of Jesus. In his mind, He believes no-one, including you, should be an stranger to the commonwealth of Israel and no longer a stranger to the Covenant of the Promise given to Abraham for all of mankind.

THE STORY OF MEPHIBOSHETH

1 Samuel 18:1-4

And it came to pass, when he had made an end of speaking unto Saul, that the soul of Jonathan was knit with the soul of David, and Jonathan loved him as his own soul. And Saul took him that day, and would let him go no more home to his father's house. Then Jonathan and David

made a covenant, because he loved him as his own soul. And Jonathan stripped himself of the robe that was upon him, and gave it to David, and his garments, even to his sword, and to his bow, and to his girdle.

The essence of entering into covenant is EXCHANGE that is to ELIMINATE THEIR WEAKNESS AND MAXIMISE THEIR STRENGTH. When they were about to enter into covenant they took an animal and cut it into two and then they would stand in the middle. Each of the parties involved would then take their Robes and hand it to the other party, then they would take the robe off the other party and put it on them then the other party on the other side would reciprocate. Jonathan demonstrates his commitment to this solemn covenant by giving David his royal robe. In a symbolic sense, (especially as this practice was understood in ancient times) in the context of covenant, David is "putting on" Jonathan. David is taking on the identity of his covenant partner Jonathan. In essence the two have become one.

Note that this new relationship heralds an end of independent living for both partners since they now are called to live for each other. There is to be a surrender of self interest for the covenant partner and we see that Jonathan willingly gave up his right to be king, ending independent living just like in the marriage covenant.

Christ the King much like Jonathan (the crown Prince), cut a new covenant in His blood with fallen mankind. When a man or woman places their faith in Christ, they become a covenant partner with Christ, entering into this new covenant in His blood.

When we enter into this new Covenant with Christ, our faithful Friend, do we also experience an exchange of robes analogous to that which occurred between Jonathan and David? Paul helps us understand the spiritual transaction that took place when we believed in Christ writing to the saints at Galatia explaining that you and I are all sons (and daughters) of God through faith in Christ Jesus.

Galatians 3:26-29

For all of you who were baptised into Christ have clothed yourselves with Christ. There is neither Jew nor Greek, there is neither slave nor free man, there is neither male

nor female; for you are all one in Christ Jesus. And if you belong to Christ, then you are Abraham's offspring, heirs according to promise.

Paul is saying that every believer has clothed themselves with Christ or has "put on" Christ, just like a soldier who belongs to an army would do to demonstrate his association and affiliation to the cause. A believer who identifies himself with Jesus Christ through faith is divinely clothed with Christ which is a sign and a symbolic way to describe Christ's life, presence, and righteous nature enveloping the believer.

Job declared that, "I put on righteousness, and it clothed me. My justice was like a robe and a turban" (see Job 29:14).

Whatever the Lord Jesus is and has, becomes the believer's. Because Christ has the love of the Father, so do we. Because Christ has full access to the Father, so do we. And because Christ has the full resources of the Father, so do we. As Jesus is, so are we in this world.

When Isaiah is prophesying and releasing the Word of the Lord in Chapter 61, he proclaims that God "has clothed (Messiah) me with garments of salvation and wrapped him with a robe of righteousness" (see Isaiah 61:10).

What happens to our old clothes when we enter this new covenant with Christ? Paul explains that "by God's doing we are in Christ Jesus, Who became to us...righteousness (see 1st Corinthians 1:30), and adds in this second letter to the Corinthians that "He made Him who knew no sin to be sin on our behalf, that we might become righteousness of God in Him" (see 2 Corinthians 5:21).

Notice that in Ephesians 4:25, Paul begins with "therefore" (which is a term used to denote a conclusion). The idea is that since at the time of salvation we have taken off our old nature and put on this brand new garment.

By doing this saints, it means supernaturally we are now empowered by the Spirit Who energises the new person we is now in Christ. From that moment onwards, we have a responsibility to daily put this new life into practice by putting off specific attitudes and actions, as described by Paul in his extensive letter to the Ephesian Church. With David & Jonathan, there is another reference to clothing in 1st Samuel 18:

And Jonathan took off the robe that was on him and gave it to David, with his armour, even to his sword and his bow and his belt.

By swapping their weaponry it signified another covenant exchange. In the context of war, it meant that:

YOUR ENEMIES ARE MY ENEMIES.
YOUR FRIENDS ARE MY FRIENDS.

In Paul's letter to the Ephesian Church, he highlights the importance of wearing the full armour of God which includes, of course, the belt of truth. The purpose of a belt is to hold our trousers up. It holds things together. It is fastened to secure our clothing and keep it in its rightful place.

Truth has this same effect. The exchange of belts symbolises one saying "I am receiving this object (the belt of truth) has the ability to hold everything in position". Jonathan was telling David, "you are going to be my covenant brother, when you are weak you can now borrow my strength and now we are in covenant". Our purpose as Kingdom Participants is to eliminate our individual weaknesses and maximise our corporate strength.

THE WALK OF DEATH

In Genesis 15, a profound exchange takes place between Abraham and God. It involves Abraham walking in blood barefooted, something many today would find ritualistic, controversial and very questionable. A personal covenant was being made between God and man, something that had never happened before. Theologians refer to this act as "the walk of death", symbolising death to independence or individual living. This was a foreshadow of what Paul was referring to when he talks about a kind of personal death in Galatians 2:

It is no longer I that lives but Christ lives in me

Now they would begin to declare and swear out loud an oath as they lift their fist and point them unto heaven saying "May the Lord do unto me as these animals if i do not keep my part of the covenant".

The whole essence of it is if you forfeit the covenant you also forfeit the right to live the life Christ has made available for us. When they seal the covenant they would talk about what they owned. Then they would cut their wrists. That was the token of covenant like the rainbow shown to Noah. They would also cut around their finger and also in a place where only those in covenant with them would see the mark (circumcision) which was the token of Abrahamic Covenant. After that, they would take dirt mixed with stone and rub it in that covenant wound. They wanted to leave a scar that could not be erased, that's why the Bible says in 2nd Timothy 2:19,

"this foundation stands secure having this seal that God knows those that are his".

This was done to remind them of the God's covenant promise which says when you see this scar, know that I will not take you off My mind. Based on the Word written in Psalms 115:12, we know that the Lord can never forget us because He has His nail wounds in His hands to remind Him of this everlasting Covenant.

Once all this was done accordingly, there would be a change of name just like the one we witness in Genesis 17:5 (Abram to Abraham & Sarai to Sarah). The significance of these particular name changes is that they both add the prefix ("Yah") connected to the name "Yah-weh" to their names. Finally, they would sit down and take bread as a Covenant token and God would be obliged to say, based on all of this, "Child, I call you My friend" just like He did with Abraham.

Isaiah 53:3 says,

"Surely he has born our grief and sorrow".

Grief and sorrow comes from two Hebrew words that is "Cholii" and "Macob". Cholii means sickness and Macob means disease. The word "borne" or "bear" is the same Hebrew word that they used to drive the

51

scapegoat out of the camp on the day of atonement, bearing their sins and never to be seen again. That means when Christ bore our sicknesses and carried our disease he was driven outside the camp to die and never to be seen again. Because of this, we know sickness has no rightful place in our bodies, you can never have a sickness of your own, because you know Christ took care of it.

God cannot make you sick to teach you something, if you think otherwise that means you do not understand Covenant. The fleshly notion of "no pain, no gain" is not true because Covenant says "I have nothing to lose and everything to gain". Many people like to quote Job 9 when they are in distress just to feel good about themselves, but they fail to understand that Job was under an inferior covenant and his fear brought upon him. We need to come out of error and into truth, Saints. The Word of God should liberate us, not imprison us.

2 Samuel 9:1-12

And David said, Is there yet any that is left of the house of Saul, that I may shew him kindness for Jonathan's sake?

And there was of the house of Saul a servant whose name was Ziba.

And when they had called him unto David, the king said unto him, Art thou Ziba? And he said, Thy servant is he. And the king said, Is there not yet any of the house of Saul, that I may shew the kindness of God unto him? And Ziba said unto the king, Jonathan hath yet a son, which is lame on his feet. And the king said unto him, Where is he? And Ziba said unto the king, Behold, he is in the house of Machir, the son of Ammiel, in Lodebar. Then king David sent, and fetched him out of the house of Machir, the son of Ammiel, from Lodebar.

Now when Mephibosheth, the son of Jonathan, the son of Saul, was come unto David, he fell on his face, and did reverence.

And David said, Mephibosheth. And he answered, Behold thy servant! And David said unto him, Fear not: for I will surely shew thee kindness for Jonathan thy father's sake, and will restore thee all the land of Saul thy father; and thou shalt eat bread at my table continually. And he bowed himself, and said, What is thy servant, that thou shouldest look upon such a dead dog as I am? Then the king called to Ziba, Saul's servant, and said unto him, I have given unto thy master's son all that pertained to Saul and to all his house.

Thou therefore, and thy sons, and thy servants, shall till the land for him, and thou shalt bring in the fruits, that thy master's son may have food to eat: but Mephibosheth thy master's son shall eat bread alway at my table. Now Ziba had fifteen sons and twenty servants. Then said Ziba unto the king, According to all that my lord the king hath commanded his servant, so shall thy servant do. As for Mephibosheth, said the king, he shall eat at my table, as one of the king's sons. And Mephibosheth had a young son, whose name was Micha. And all that dwelt in the house of Ziba were servants unto Mephibosheth.

The story of Mephibosheth is such an interesting one because it is full of signs and symbols of our overall topic. The nurse that would have carried, nursed and taken of this child Mephiboseth was a stranger to the Covenant and would have had no idea that this child's father Jonathan had made a covenant with King David. She ended up dropping him and crippling him due to what I would guess was a sad combination of negligence and ignorance. In the same manner, if a pastor does not know the truth about the Covenant and is careless with the Word, they will keep you broke, sick, terrified and even crippled!

Please note that Mephibosheth did not receive healing of his legs but was still welcomed at the table. It doesn't matter what your present situation is, just like Mephibosheth was covered by the tablecloth and no one noticed that he was lame, God's grace has the ability to hide your flaws and cover you too.

Through extensive theological analysis, we see that David represents a "type" of Christ which is why this story helps to illustrates how Christ redeems a person that is in a covenant agreement with Him. In Verse 7 he says "fear not".

The absence of knowledge when it comes to the topic of covenant always leaves us afraid and uncertain of our future as Believers. We fear what we do not understand

and what we feel we cannot control. Instead of understanding our identity as sons, we continue to struggle and make slow progress when we have all the benefits of the Kingdom right in front of us. The table is there for us to have a seat but we do not know who we are! God's promises are yeah and amen. He never says no to His children, especially when we are in alignment with his Divine Will.

God has already made available everything we need for life and Godliness. He made all things available! All things! His Grace is all we need to fulfil His agenda for us here on Earth but just like Mephibosheth we can go about living a mediocre, ineffective life while our seat remains empty at the King's High Table. Believers, it is time we stopped perishing due to lack of knowledge. It is time to receive what is ours!

You will never know the Bible until you know Jesus.

UNDERSTANDING THE OLD AND NEW COVENANT IN CHRIST

You will never know the Bible until you know Jesus.

Luke 24:44-45

Then He said to them, "These are the words which I spoke to you while I was still with you, that all things must be fulfilled which were written in the Law of Moses and the Prophets and the Psalms concerning Me." And He opened their understanding, that they might comprehend the Scriptures.

JESUS CHRIST, THE FULFILMENT OF ALL SCRIPTURE

Moses was trying to describe 'Jesus' but because of his scriptural status at that time, he couldn't, then they had to work with types and shadows, such as the Blood on the door post, the Brazen Serpent, the Ark of the

Covenant, the Priestly Garment, the Tabernacle all these having a significance where new testament revelation of Christ Jesus is concerned.

John 5:39

You carefully study the Scriptures. You think that they give you eternal life. These same Scriptures tell about me!

In the above Scripture, Jesus is clearly stating that the Scriptures testify and provide evidence of His Person. Saints, Jesus is the overriding message of the Scriptures. Everything points back to Him! Praise God!

Luke 24:15-27

While they were talking, discussing these things, Jesus himself came near and walked with them. (But the two men were not allowed to recognise Jesus.) He asked them, "What's this I hear you discussing with each other as you walk?" The two men stopped, their faces looking very sad. The one named Cleopas said, "You must be the only person in Jerusalem who doesn't know what has just happened there." Jesus said, "What are you talking about?" They said, "It's about Jesus, the one from

Nazareth. To God and to all the people he was a great prophet. He said and did many powerful things. But our leaders and the leading priests handed him over to be judged and killed. They nailed him to a cross. We were hoping that he would be the one to free Israel. But then all this happened. "And now something else: It has been three days since he was killed, but today some of our women told us an amazing thing. Early this morning they went to the tomb where the body of Jesus was laid. But they did not find his body there. They came and told us they had seen some angels in a vision. The angels told them Jesus was alive! So some of our group went to the tomb too. It was just as the women said. They saw the tomb, but they did not see Jesus." Then Jesus said to the two men, "You are foolish and slow to realise what is true. You should believe everything the prophets said. The prophets said the Messiah must suffer these things before he begins his time of glory." Then he began to explain everything that had been written about himself in the Scriptures. He started with the books of Moses and then he talked about what the prophets had said about him.

They were talking about Him, yet they did not know Him. You can be preaching about Jesus and not know Him. The Bible says beginning with Moses (the first five books of the Bible) and all the Prophets, Jesus began to reveal everything concerning Himself. By saying the prophets, Jesus would have gone through the books written by Ezekiel, Daniel, Joel, Jeremiah, Micah and many others.

All of these men were trying to relate that 'Jesus would suffer these things' but could not say it because of their status and their inability to see the full picture. So the best way was to use symbols, types and shadows. Outside of Jesus, we have no message.

Dr. Abel Damina on his message on Grace mentioned that "if your interpretation of the scripture is wrong, your application is wrong. Your practice will be wrong, and your results will be wrong".

Knowing Jesus in Scripture is your remedy for all your needs. Peter was with Jesus but it took Paul to teach Him about Jesus, yet Paul never saw Jesus because revelation is better than experience.

2 Peter 3:16

...As also in all his epistles, speaking in them of these things, in which are some things hard to understand, which untaught and unstable people twist to their own destruction, as they do also the rest of the Scriptures.

AN ACCURATE BREAKDOWN OF SCRIPTURE

As you can see, even Peter, one of the closest disciples to Jesus, acknowledged that the revelation given to Paul was, for lack of a better term, "hard to understand". As ministers preaching the Word today, we must also acknowledge that if you cannot interpret the Bible correctly, you will not be able to teach it and produce any results. So when we use the term Scriptures, what the Bible is referring to is Genesis to Malachi which is also known as the Mystery, Matthew to Revelations is the revelation of the Mystery.

The New Testament does not include Matthew, Mark, Luke, and John because they are HISTORICAL BOOKS revealing the humanity of Christ.

Can I suggest to you that the Old Testament also does not technically include Genesis, either, as this was a historically prophetic account of how creation took place and how the first families of the earth came about. The testimony of the Old Covenant begins with the introduction of the Law, which takes place in Exodus.

Within the historical books revealing the humanity of Christ, this is the only place where you read that Jesus wept, was tired, and was hungry. Simply because the focus from the authors was more on the human nature of Jesus rather than the divine nature of Christ. So, until the blood was shed, there was no true New Testament. The New Testament is a by-product of the shed blood of Christ. In the four Gospels no blood was shed until the end of the Gospel of John, which means the beginning of the New Testament is in the book recording the Acts of the Apostles.

So, if we teach from the four Gospels alone, it will cause foundational principles to be ignored and not addressed fully. We need to focus on the other books that follow the Gospels so that there is a healthy balance of both the historical and doctrinal portions of the Word.

Hebrews 9:15-16

So Christ brings a new agreement from God to his people. He brings this agreement so that those who are chosen by God can have the blessings God promised, blessings that last forever. This can happen only because Christ died to free people from sins committed against the commands of the first agreement. When someone dies and leaves a will, there must be proof that the one who wrote the will is dead. "where there is a testament there must be a death of the testator ..."

Until Jesus died there was no New Testament.

Hebrews 8:7-9

If there was nothing wrong with the first agreement, then there would be no need for a second agreement. But

64

God found something wrong with the people. He said, "The time is coming, says the Lord, when I will give a new agreement to the people of Israel and to the people of Judah. It will not be like the agreement that I gave to their fathers. That is the agreement I gave when I took them by the hand and led them out of Egypt. They did not continue following the agreement I gave them, and I turned away from them", says the Lord.

Romans 16:25

Praise God! He is the one who can make you strong in faith. He can use the Good News that I teach to make you strong. It is the message of Jesus Christ that I tell people. That message is the secret truth that was hidden for ages and ages but has been made known.

Remember this Saints,

THE OLD TESTAMENT IS JESUS <u>CONCEALED</u>
THE NEW TESTAMENT IS JESUS <u>REVEALED</u>

The Old Testament is the Scripture concealed as a document of types, metaphors, shadows and mysteries.

The Old Testament gives to us a portfolio of promises and prophecies. The New Testament, however, is the revealed reality of those types, shadows, promises and prophecies. The New Testament is the revelation (or revealing) of everything hidden within those mysteries.

Mark 4:11

Jesus said, "Only you can know the secret truth about God's Kingdom. But to those other people I tell everything by using stories.

To understand the Old Testament, we need to see things from a New Testament perspective, to really know the truth behind it.

Hebrews 9:15

"And for this cause he is the mediator of the new testament, that by means of death,...they which are called might receive the promise of eternal inheritance."

The Old Testament is the forerunner of the New, the principles outlined within the text show this to us very clearly. The Bible teaches us the reality of Christ through two Testaments, the Old Testament & the

New. In our imagination, we assume they are complements, or even supplements. The Old Testament is rightly called old because it is outdated and expired. It was never designed to bring salvation. Rather, it was given to us as a roadmap that directs us towards it.

Reading the Word from an old Covenant perspective never provided, and never will provide, a doorway to righteousness through Christ Jesus. Instead, it shows us the impact and danger of not having a right standing with God. In addition to that, the Law operates on a system of conditional blessings. The Law is a demand for performance, while grace is a supply of help. Jesus warned about putting new wine into old wineskins:

Mark 2:22

"...else the new wine doth burst the bottles, and the wine is spilled, and the bottles will be marred: but new wine must be put into new bottles."

How often do we fall into this trap! We practice both Testaments simultaneously, ignoring the truth that one has in fact replaced the other. Everything has changed and by everything, this includes our walk with Christ, our cultural trends and tendencies, our relationships, our worship, our service and prayer to God and the way we live our lives on a daily basis. Attempting to mix expired practices with new ones will always produce a bad end result. Sadly, this is the norm today in many churches. But hear the words of Paul as he writes to the Corinthian church,

2 Corinthians 3:5-6

"Not that we are sufficient of ourselves to think of any thing as being from ourselves, but our sufficiency is from God, who also hath made us able ministers of the new testament; not of the letter, but of the spirit: for the letter killeth, but the spirit giveth life."

Our sufficiency is from God. And this is possible because of the reality of the new covenant in Christ Jesus. Clearly, we now have a clear distinction of what both Testaments provide,

~~Death~~ vs Life,

~~Condemnation~~ vs Righteousness,

~~Flesh~~ vs Spirit

Hebrews 8:10

I will put My laws in their mind and write them on their hearts

God was not referring to the Ten Commandments, known as the laws of the old covenant, since He said that He found fault with that covenant and declared it obsolete.

2 Corinthians 3:3-8

You show that you are a letter from Christ that he sent through us. This letter is not written with ink but with the Spirit of the living God. It is not written in stone tablets but on human hearts. We can say this because through Christ we feel sure before God. I don't mean that we are able to do anything good ourselves. It is God who makes us able to do all that we do. He made us able to be servants of a new agreement from himself to his people. It is not an agreement of written laws, but it is of the Spirit. The written law brings death, but the Spirit gives life. The old agreement that brought death, written with words on stone, came with God's glory. In fact, the face of Moses was so bright with glory (a glory that was ending)

that the people of Israel could not continue looking at his face. So surely the new agreement that comes from the life-giving Spirit has even more glory.

There are epistles and testaments, one is written by human hands with ink and the other is imprinted by the Spirit. For the Old Testament, its content is inscribed on stone, while for the other, it is imprinted on the human heart. The quality of revelation you carry is what determines your level of power and authority, especially in the realm of the spirit. The height of your dimension within your spiritual capabilities is decided by what testament your revelation originates from. If you operate from a religious, works-based belief system, your results will show it. Under the Law, man is in charge but under Grace, no one takes the glory but God. Jesus came to correct all Moses had said. 2 Corinthians 3:16 informs us that when someone turns and follows the Lord, the veil that once blinding them is taken away. As long as you are still preaching or reading Moses (the Law) you are under a veil. Because of this veil, many are still preaching bondage, emphasising on sin and work-based faith. All these things are established after the

Ten Commandments, thereby binding people with a doctrine that has passed on. God himself in the Old Testament corrected what Moses had said concerning that. To summarise, let us look at the three laws that complete the New Covenant of Grace:

The First Law: The Law of Love

Matthew 22:37–40

Jesus said to him, "'You shall love the Lord your God with all your heart, with all your soul, and with all your mind.' This is the first and great commandment. And the second is like it: 'You shall love your neighbour as yourself.' On these two commandments hang all the Law and the Prophets."

The Second Law: Law of Liberty

James 1:25

But he who looks into the perfect law of liberty and continues in it, and is not a forgetful hearer but a doer of the work, this one will be blessed in what he does.

The Third Law: Law of Faith

Romans 3:27

Where is boasting then? It is excluded. By what law? Of works? No, but by the law of faith.

These are the laws of the new covenant. You live according to the laws of the new covenant when you are conscious of how much God loves you. And the more you are conscious of His love for you, the more your heart is filled with love. When that happens, you will love God and the people around you supernaturally and effortlessly. That is God writing on your heart the royal law of love—that we love because He first loved us.

1 John 4:19

We love Him because He first loved us.

Romans 5:5

Now hope does not disappoint, because the love of God has been poured out in our hearts by the Holy Spirit who was given to us.

Faith always begins at the point of the known will of God

THE SURETY OF THE COVENANT

Faith always begins at the point of the known will of God

Faith cannot go past the question mark. If you have to question whether or not God is going to do it, your faith has been paralysed. Faith always begins at the point of the KNOWN WILL OF GOD. The access to true covenant faith is understanding, because it is impossible to doubt what you understand. Fear, doubt and unbelief always resides in the areas where you are ignorant and the root of prejudice is ignorance.

God is more impressed by faith than He is with your ability to perform. Abraham believed God and it was accounted unto him righteousness. Abraham wanted to know how God was going to do it for him, he wanted to be certain. In Genesis 22, Abraham the man who couldn't get a child was at this point able to kill him because something happened for him to start believing. Abraham had known and understood that God himself would provide the sacrifice because he is both the Initiator and Administrator of this Covenant.

God had to make Abraham understand the concept of covenant first in order for it to be easy for him to believe God. Hebrews 11 states that Abraham had seen (in a vision) that his son would be raised from the dead. This gave him the confidence and the assurance that this same God who had given him his son was more than able to raise him up again and bring him back to life. He understood that in the covenant you don't ask your partner to do more for you than He is prepared to do for you.

God asked Abraham to bring all five items for the covenant to work; these were the prominent types and shadows of the new testaments doctrine where redemption is concerned. Numbers 19 shows that a red heifer represents a cleansing and sanctification of people before they are ready to see God. In Genesis 22, the ram is a symbol of God's atoning grace. It acts as a sign that God would provide a sacrifice to release us from our sins. In Leviticus, we understand that on the Day of Atonement they had to bring a three year old goat. The priest would pronounce a curse on it and it would be sent outside the city, in the same way that Christ took our curses and was driven outside the city to die. The pigeon and the turtle doves represent a redemptive sacrifice for the poor people who couldn't defend themselves.

The pieces had to be torn and divided, thus why Jesus was bruised for our iniquities (see Hebrews 10:19-20). As I mentioned before in the earlier chapters, I want to recap the process of the covenant just for you to appreciate its seriousness.

In Abraham's society, when two families made covenant together, they gave to one another everything they had and all they represented. They were no longer two, but one. Families bound themselves together in blood agreements in order to fill in the gaps created by each other's weaknesses and needs. Where the first tribe was strong, the second was weak. Where the second tribe was strong, the first was weak. Together, they were both strong. These two families drew up the terms of their agreement and discussed them until each article was fully and mutually agreeable. Then they chose representatives and a place to cut the covenant. As they prepared for the solemn ceremony, at least three large animals were sacrificed. Their carcasses were split down the spine, and the halves were placed on the ground opposite each other. The result was a trail of blood between the halves. This path was called "the way of blood."

When the covenant ceremony began, the two representatives exchanged their coats. This signifying the mutual exchange of authority. By this act the covenant representatives was saying, "All that I do, all that I have is now yours." Next the covenant representatives exchanged their weapons. Through this they were saying, "My strength is now your strength. Your enemies are now my enemies." After the coats and weapons were exchanged, then came the walk of blood. Twice the representatives walked through "the way of blood," stopping in the centre. There they pronounced their pledges of loyalty, making promises to each other that could never be broken. This pronouncement was called "the blessing of the covenant."

A curse was also pronounced. The curse was the penalty for breaking the terms of the agreement they swore by their god, thereby making him third party to the covenant.

Next came the cutting of the covenant. The representatives cut their hands and wrists and bound their wrists together so that their blood would intermingle. After their loyalty was sworn to each other, the families joined their names together as a permanent sign that they had become one. Finally, they ate a covenant meal of bread and wine together. The bread signified their flesh, and the wine signified their blood. The covenant meal represented their willingness and commitment to lay down their lives for each other. So when Abraham laid his son down on the altar of sacrifice, he opened the way for God—his covenant partner—to do the same thing with His only Son, Jesus, on the cross years later. But here's an important point for you to realise: Jesus didn't just appear on the scene at that time. He'd been involved in that covenant from the very beginning. He is the Alpha and Omega, the Beginning and the End, the First and the Last. He has fashioned all things from the very beginning of time eternity and all things were made through Him, for Him and because of Him. Saints, everything about our Lord is strategic, creative and intentional!

According to Galatians 3:16, while God was binding Himself in covenant to Abraham on earth, He was also making covenant with Jesus in heaven.

Galatians 3:16

"Now to Abraham and his seed were the promises made. He saith not, And to seeds, as of many; but as of one, And to thy seed, which is Christ."

Abraham was the earthly representative. Jesus was the heavenly representative. The covenant was not only between God and Abraham, but between God the Father and God the Son. By making covenant with Jesus, He was making covenant with someone He knew would never break it, thereby removing the need for a curse. The important question is, how does all this apply to you and me?

Galatians 3:29 is the binding tie. "And if ye be Christ's, then are ye Abraham's seed, and heirs according to the promise."

We are the unborn generations who looked on as God cut the covenant with Abraham, the father of our Covenant faith. Romans 8:17 calls us joint heirs with Jesus Christ. Through the new covenant, God has promised to care for us the same way He would love and care for Jesus.

This new covenant is better than the old. If you'll read Deuteronomy 28, you'll find the blessings that are promised to those who keep the terms of the agreement. They're wonderful promises—it's hard to imagine any better. But keep reading and you'll also find the curse that will fall on those who break the agreement. That's where our covenant differs.

Although we ourselves have been guilty of breaking the terms of the covenant, we've been freed from the penalty of it. Jesus was not only the blood sacrifice, but He also became our Representative—the one Mediator between God and man!

1 John 2:1

We have an advocate with the Father, Jesus Christ the righteous.

He not only sees to our forgiveness when we confess our sins, He cleanses us from all unrighteousness. Jesus was not only the blood sacrifice and the representative, He was also the covenant meal.

John 6:51

"I am the living bread which came down from heaven: if any man eat of this bread, he shall live for ever: and the bread that I will give is my flesh, which I will give for the life of the world"

When you understand covenant terminology, then you can see the thread of a covenant relationship woven all through the New Testament.

Read Ephesians 6:10-11 and 13-17 in this new light:

Finally, my brethren, be strong in the Lord, and in the power of his might. Put on the whole armour of God, that ye may be able to stand against the wiles of the devil.

Wherefore take unto you the whole armour of God, that ye may be able to withstand in the evil day, and having done all, to stand. Stand therefore, having your loins girt about with truth, and having on the breastplate of righteousness; and your feet shod with the preparation of the gospel of peace; above all, taking the shield of faith, wherewith ye shall be able to quench all the fiery darts of the wicked. And take the helmet of salvation, and the sword of the Spirit, which is the word of God.

Jesus has exchanged His weapons and armour with you and made you strong in the power of His might. He exchanged your weakness for His strength. Through a covenant relationship, you are now one with Him. Jesus took your sin and gave you His robe of righteousness and right-standing with God. He has become so totally one with you that He has given you the authority to use His Name.

Mark 16:17

"And these signs shall follow them that believe; In my name shall they cast out devils"

The devil has no right to interfere in your affairs. The new covenant does not depend on your ability to keep it. It depends on Jesus' ability to keep it. Just like with Abraham and similarly with David, you have a covenant with Almighty God through Jesus Christ. Just like Abraham, you can become fully persuaded that what God has promised you, He is able also to perform. Just like David, you can stand on that covenant and whip any uncircumcised circumstance that stands in your way—no matter how big it looks.

Friend, it is imperative that you understand that our covenant in Christ is better. It doesn't carry a curse anymore. Right now, open your Bible and read Deuteronomy 28:16-68. That's the list of curses Christ has freed you from. They include every diabolical thing the devil could ever use to destroy you. Read them and rejoice! Those are the things God has healed you of and delivered you from. Let me encourage you today, receive your deliverance. Receive your healing. Jesus paid the price for it. He bore the curse. He became the covenant sacrifice for you, proving once and for all just how intensely He desires to love and to bless you. From the time Jesus was born until He went to Calvary, He never broke the terms of the covenant. Yet when He went to the Cross, He bore the curse, or penalty, for breaking it. Why? So that you and I would never have to bear it.

Galatians 3:13-14

"Christ hath redeemed us from the curse of the law, being made a curse for us: for it is written, Cursed is every one that hangeth on a tree: that the blessing of Abraham might come on the Gentiles through Jesus Christ; that we might receive the promise of the Spirit through faith"

We are no longer under the old covenant of law, but under the new covenant of grace. Unfortunately, many Christians are not established in this truth. They don't really understand how Jesus' death and resurrection have placed them in the new covenant, and made the old covenant obsolete.

The difference, and it is major is that under the Old Covenant, those who trusted God in regard to the Law could not be born again like we are under the New Covenant. Their new birth could not take place until

Jesus died for their sins, was raised from the dead and glorified. Before these events happened, another provision was in place. When Old Covenant believers died, they were held or preserved in a place the Bible calls "Paradise" until the work of redemption was completed. In this sense of the word, they were saved; however, they did not receive the promise of the new birth until after the Messiah paid the price for man's redemption, But when Jesus went to the cross, that all changed.

Hebrews 10:14 tells us,

"For by a single offering He has forever completely cleansed and perfected those who are consecrated and made holy".

Justification, right-standing with God and the new birth are attained only by faith in the blood of Jesus (see Romans 3:21-26). They are not attained by keeping the Law because Christ is the end of the Law (see Romans 10:4).

After Jesus made the sacrifice for sin conclusively on the cross and was raised from the dead, Ephesians 4:8 states that He ascended on high and "led captivity captive." This speaks of those Old Covenant believers who were being held in the place called Paradise. He took the Good News to them that they could receive the benefit of His sacrifice and be born again. They believed the Gospel and went from Paradise to Heaven!

The blood of Jesus not only atoned for our sins; it was completely wiped out, as if it was never there. The Hebrew word "atone" means "to cover over" or "to make up for". In the Old Covenant, the priesthood covered or atoned for the sins of the Israelites—the breaking of the Law—through the shedding of the blood of animals.

The moment we make Jesus our Lord, we enter into a Blood-covenant relationship with God. All that the Father has, He turned over to Jesus in the New Covenant (see John 16:15). We become joint-heirs with Jesus in what we call a New Birth experience (see Romans 8:17). Because of this, God's riches and His very best (in every sense of the word) becomes ours to enjoy, to share with others and to impart on those who need it the most!

Jeremiah 31:31-32

"Behold, the days are coming, declares the LORD, when I will make a new covenant with the house of Israel and the house of Judah, not like the covenant that I made with their fathers on the day when I took them by the hand to bring them out of the land of Egypt..."

A covenant is a compact or binding agreement between persons, with stipulations and promises. The book of Hebrews clearly teaches us that Christ established his New Covenant, which is distinct from the old one. "He takes away the first in order to establish the second". The Old Covenant (Testament) is now "obsolete", praise God! Jesus ended the Old Testament Law by "nailing it to the cross" (see Colossians 2:14).

His "once for and for all" Sacrifice is superior to the temporary, imperfect sacrifices once done under the Law. His Grace abounds so much more! Now let's take a look at faith and how knowledge and acceptance of this New Covenant elevates to a higher realm of faith where anything, and I mean anything, is possible.

'This Gospel does not demand Faith, it is Faith'

COVENANT FAITH

'This Gospel does not demand Faith, it is Faith'

1 Corinthians 15:1-4

"Moreover, brethren, I declare to you the gospel which I preached to you, which also you received and in which you stand, by which also you are saved, if you hold fast that word which I preached to you—unless you believed in vain. For I delivered to you first of all that which I also received: that Christ died for our sins according to the Scriptures, and that He was buried, and that He rose again the third day according to the Scriptures."

A WORD ON FAITH

Paul says this is the Gospel about what he received. This was the message of Paul. This gospel does not demand Faith, it is Faith. It generates faith within the life of the believer. The Gospel is the Word of faith.

1. It bring faith
2. It saves
3. It is power. (for I am not ashamed of the Gospel for it is the power ...)

The believer does not need their own work-based faith. In fact, the reason you are called a believer is because in order for you to be saved, you would have had to already possess a significant measure of faith. The Gospel of Jesus has true, effective power. That is why when a man or woman of God preaches with conviction, truth and full knowledge of the Authority of the Kingdom, creative miracles become the norm, signs and wonders follow, hearts are convicted, demons are expelled, minds are changed, and healing takes place.

We cannot receive faith when we ask for faith, simply because we would not have been able to receive the original Message of the Cross without it in the first place!

The Message we received is the Message of faith in itself. When the message is received, faith is released!

So, for us to believe for something then ask to have faith for it is a misunderstanding and a contradiction. The Scriptures we mostly quote about faith are from the Gospels in which Jesus was speaking to non-believers. Remember now that the Gospels are books of account, and at this stage, Jesus was still teaching people with an Old Testament mentality, whose minds were embedded with the idea that you had to use your own works if you wanted to get anything from God. This is the reason he would say to them "your faith has made you whole". But remember John says,

John 20:31

"...but these are written that you may believe that Jesus is the Christ, the Son of God, and that believing you may have life in His name."

The Epistles are the books that were written for us that believe.

1 John 5:13

" These things I have written to you who believe in the name of the Son of God, that you may know that you have

eternal life, and that you may continue to believe in the name of the Son of God"

A believer in Jesus cannot have a faith problem, instead, they may have a knowledge deficiency. The reason the Word is preached to us consistently is that so that we may know that we have in Christ. The Epistles are written so that we may know.

The Gospels were written so that the unbelievers may believe. The Old Testament is a relationship between God and I, powered by my ability to work hard and labour as I attempt to please God. Meanwhile, the New Testament is about what Christ has done that has pleased God already. Now, the only thing that pleases the Father is my faith and my acceptance of what His Son is already done.

When you understand what the Blood has achieved, you have understood the New Testament. His Blood has forgiven my sin. Once you fully comprehend what this means for you, your family, your health, your business, your ministry and for all of humanity, you have officially understood the New Testament and can now be a participant in the Kingdom of God.

Hebrews 10:12

"But this Man, after He had offered one sacrifice for sins forever, sat down at the right hand of God..."

His blood paid for the sin past, present and future. That is the gospel we preach. When Moses said "show me the glory," he was not asking for money or miracles because he was already wealth and performed miracles in Egypt.

Haggai 2:6-7

"This is what the Lord All-Powerful said, 'In just a little while, I will once again shake things up. I will shake heaven and earth, and I will shake the sea and the dry land. 7 I will shake up the nations, and they will come to you with wealth from every nation. And then I will fill this Temple with glory.' That is what the Lord All-Powerful said!"

Moses was asking for permission to participate in what have right now, the New Testament, the finished works of Christ, the promises and benefits, the glory, riches and endless inheritance of the House of God.

Colossians 1:25-27

"1 became a servant of the church because God gave me a special work to do. This work helps you. My work is to tell the complete message of God. This message is the secret truth that was hidden since the beginning of time. It was hidden from everyone for ages, but now it has been made known to God's holy people. God decided to let his people know just how rich and glorious that truth is. That secret truth, which is for all people, is that Christ lives in you, his people. He is our hope for glory".

Your body is the home (or temple) of the Holy Ghost. The Holy Ghost in the man is God's glory (His majesty, weightiness and goodness) made manifest. So the entire Glory of God is in a house. This is the treasure in earthen vessels we have often read about but failed to understand.

Galatians 1:11-12

"Brothers and sisters, 1 want you to know that the Good News message 1 told you was not made up by anyone. 1

did not get my message from any other human. The Good
News is not something I learned from other people. Jesus
Christ himself gave it to me. He showed me the Good
News that I should tell people."

Paul wrote this book first and it was a book of defence
of his message of Grace. This message was a revelation.
Paul wrote of the intrinsic details of what happened to
Jesus in his death. There was no way that anyone knew
what happened to Jesus when he went to blot out the
handwriting of the enemy and disarmed them.

The Gospels (according to Matthew, Mark, Luke &
John) point to what happened in the events before and
after He died and also what happened when He rose.
The Epistles, however, give us insight into what would
have happened during the three days between His burial and His resurrection. As Paul writes these Epistles,
we also receive revelation and clarity on the reality and
consequences of His resurrection.

The Good News Message we all need to hear is not
just about a historical figure "who went about doing
good", it is about a Man's Death, Burial and

Resurrection. 1st Corinthians 15:14-19 tells us, if we just preach death and resurrection we have missed the vital concepts of the Gospel. Religion will teach you death and resurrection only. But we also preach the burial because this is when we disarmed the principalities and powers and took the keys of Hades and death. The secret to the rights that were bought by the Blood that was shed, is also found in the time-space before the resurrection took place. Your greatness is measured by the revelation you have. If we are to walk in the power, dominion and authority that belongs to us in Christ, we have to do better in understanding where that power originates from.

'Faith is not mental but a spiritual force'

LIVING WITHOUT A COVENANT

'Faith is not mental but a spiritual force'

1 Corinthians 1:18

"The teaching about the cross seems foolish to those who are lost. But to us who are being saved it is the power of God." to them that perish, the teaching of THE CROSS is foolishness, but UNTO US, it is the power of God.

1 Corinthians 15:1–3

"Now, brothers and sisters, I want you to remember the Good News I told you. You received that Good News message, and you continue to base your life on it. That Good News, the message you heard from me, is God's way to save you. But you must continue believing it. If you don't, you believed for nothing. I gave you the message that I received. I told you the most important truths: that Christ died for our sins, as the Scriptures say"

These two Scriptures outline the Gospel that you received and it is the foundation from which you stand. This Good News gives you a stance, it secures you and assures you of the Promise given to you through Christ. This is all in existence because Christ died for our sins, was buried and triumphantly rose again after just three days.

1 Corinthians 15:14

"And if Christ has never been raised, then the message we tell is worth nothing. And your faith is worth nothing". If it does not include this, then it is in vain.

Romans 10:14

But before people can pray to the Lord for help, they must believe in him. And before they can believe in the Lord, they must hear about him. And for anyone to hear about the Lord, someone must tell them.

For one to be truly saved there must be a Person in "WHOM" we believe. The power and effectiveness of the Gospel must be based on our belief in Him, for salvation is found in a Person, salvation exists because of the sacrificial love of one Man. It is not based on mere philosophy, theology or mentality.

That is why the Gospel does not just demand faith, it supplies Faith. It is why it is called the Message of Faith. Once again friends, faith is not mental, it is a spiritual force. Faith is not a thing, it is a Person and that Person is Jesus Christ. Not only is He the author and finisher of our faith, as Covenant believers we could say He is our faith.

JESUS IS OUR FAITH

You cannot ask a woman to be a woman, neither could you ask a lion to be a lion. It is what it is. We are who we are, and we cannot struggle to be it once it is in line with our natural origin.

In the same way, when you hear the Message of Christ, faith is released and its power is activated within our hearts. Faith comes by hearing the pure Message of Jesus. We don't have to struggle to have this faith, we do not need to strive for it. All we have to do is to acknowledge it and allow it to do its work.

Romans 10:17

So faith comes from hearing the Good News. And people hear the Good News when someone tells them about Christ.

Please be reminded that you are called a believer because you have faith, not necessarily because you are saved. Yes, you may be saved but remember that faith is the ultimate prerequisite. Salvation comes through a decision and a confession based on the faith (belief that Jesus died, was buried and resurrected for you and I) that has already been released. Once faith comes, it cannot go. When you got saved, you were truly saved, it cannot come gradually. Salvation may be a gradual process but it a one time deal. Salvation is only once, when you receive the Message, you are saved once and for all. The Message produces and generates faith in you.

Mark 11:22-24 tells us to have God's level of faith. This is the power of faith that can be put to use to achieve anything. When this level of faith is put to work it can literally relocate mountains. Jesus was not lying, neither was He exaggerating. It is impossible for

Him to lie. So what level of faith was He referring to? My answer is it is a kind of faith that is not natural to the human kind. It is a level of faith that is fully dependant on the power and sovereign nature of God as Creator of the entire Universe, including all living things on earth, above earth and even below. This level of faith is a kind of faith that is reliant on the all-powerful nature of God. It is a faith that knows nothing can deny the Creator of His will and agenda.

"If you say to this mountain and you don't doubt, you will have what you say".

Not what God says. True Faith has productivity that cannot be denied. In this conversation, Jesus teaches his disciples to have the "God Kind of Faith", or the faith of God. In other words, the kind of faith that God has. This is a level of faith in God that is unattainable for most but not impossible to achieve. Remember this all happened in a time of transition from the old covenant to the new, because Jesus had not died yet, so none of the them had the faith of Jesus. This new level of faith was not birthed in them yet, Jesus was merely painting the picture of what they could achieve if they believed on this level.

When a person is born-again, they are born again because they have come to Faith.

When you're born again you are reborn by faith because the message of Christ brought faith in you. The acceptance of Christ requires faith on the inside before the benefits of that decision can manifest on the outside. That means the DNA of a New Testament believer is faith constituted, that's why we are called believers because we already have faith. In the Gospels Jesus would say words like "your faith has made you whole", but now in the New Testament because we are coming from a position of faith, He says in James, "the prayers of a believer heals the sick". It's no longer your effort but God's finished work that does the job. All you need is to be in sync with the God Kind of Faith.

Salvation does not bring a change of lifestyle. Christianity is not character modification. The experience of salvation that leads to true Christianity is an encounter that gives you a brand new life and an end to all blood curses, because you become a completely new species with no history ever established before. This is the miracle of salvation. This new life now has its own character, it gives you a completely new genetic blueprint and allows you to benefit from the grace and gifts (charisma) of God through Jesus Christ.

The good nature of God is embodied in the character of Christ that we now have access to. These character traits are known as the fruit of the Holy Spirit (see Galatians 5:22). The "charisma" (divinely conferred power) are what we know as the gifts of the Holy Spirit (see 1st Corinthians 12).

Access to both are required a full life of God's presence, glory and power. So while your personality, preferences and tendencies are not automatically modified or altered, you do have a brand new character and holy nature in Christ, which now manifest themselves as love, joy, peace, gentleness, patience, goodness, kindness, faithfulness and self control. Anything other than this, points us to a situation where we are looking into the wrong mirror. Let's see what James says about this:

James 1:23-24

For if anyone is a hearer of the word and not a doer, he is like a man observing his natural face in a mirror; for he observes himself, goes away, and immediately forgets what kind of man he was.

When we look into our mirrors, instantly we are led to make adjustments because of the flaws we immediately notice about ourselves. Spending enough time in front of that mirror allows us to see exactly what is right, and exactly what is wrong with our appearance. When we rush, however, it is much easier to miss something and leave without knowing what we look like. Think of a stain you miss or a button you forget to do. In the same way, when we rush the process of self-evaluation, time with the Holy Spirit and devotion to the Word of God, we are easily deceived and forced into making "corrections" we do not need, simply because we do not truly know what we look like ourselves. This leads to instances like when people say that you need deliverance when really all you need is some counselling. In parts of the world, this frequent misjudgement often leads people to suggest you visit a witch doctor when all you need is some time alone for fasting and prayer.

When we do not know what we look like, we fall into traps that were never supposed to affect us. This is what what happens when we are just hearers of the Word and not doers. When we have the knowledge of Christ, that knowledge surpasses everything: fearful imaginations, bad reports, negative words, curses, evil thoughts and anything that does not exalt the will of God and the reality of His finished work. We believe wholeheartedly that we don't fight for victory, we fight from victory. The difference between life in the Old Testament and life in the New is that <u>we are born again</u>.

No one in the Old Testament was born again. Moses was not born again. Elisha, Adam, Enoch couldn't have been born again before Christ went on the Cross. The message of the Cross is the power unto salvation, without it there is no salvation or eternal life. The patriarchs and pioneers we know of in the Old Testament believed in a promissory note. They did not experience full access to what we have access to today in Christ. They didn't have the substance of the richness of God's Holy Spirit. While we now have full entry into the throne room of God's grace, they had shadows, they did not enjoy that reality. This is why when they died was no entry into heaven. Heaven couldn't come to man and man couldn't go to heaven because there was a barrier between heaven and earth.

Hebrew 11:1

"Now faith is the substance of things hoped for, the evidence of things not seen.

Hebrews 11 is the famous Scripture we all use to describe the concept of faith. While this verse maintains its validity and weight, we have to move beyond the elementary teaching of this verse and strive towards a higher level of understanding, revelation and interpretation. Our faith relies on this. This level of faith was what the Old Testament people operated from but that is not the same level we should operate from today. Substance of things hoped for. This is the faith they used before Jesus came, so their faith was sustained by a hope of things that never materialised.

Hebrews 11:39

"And all these, having obtained a good testimony through faith, did not receive the promise," they received not the promise. So who are these people?

Note that they did not receive the promise as this was faith based on hope.

Hebrews 11:3-5

Faith helps us understand that God created the whole world by his command. This means that the things we see were made by something that cannot be seen. Cain and Abel both offered sacrifices to God. But Abel offered a better sacrifice to God because he had faith. God said he was pleased with what Abel offered. And so God called him a good man because he had faith. Abel died, but through his faith he is still speaking. Enoch was carried away from this earth, so he never died. The Scriptures tell us that before he was carried off, he was a man who pleased God. Later, no one knew where he was, because God had taken Enoch to be with him. This all happened because he had faith.

In verse 3, the term "worlds" refers to the worlds of people like Noah, Moses, Job & the Prophets.

Hebrews 11:13

All these great people continued living with faith until they died. They did not get the things God promised his people. But they were happy just to see those promises coming far in the future. They accepted the fact that they were like visitors and strangers here on earth.

DEVELOPING A NEW COVENANT MENTALITY

'Faith is the life and lifestyle of a believer'

When you come to Jesus, you have come to faith (remember Jesus is our faith). You have not only come to faith, you have embraced completed faith. He is the author, perfecter and finisher of our faith. Faith in Jesus is not partial, based on hope or hopeful. It is complete, perfected and effective. Faith is not a tool. This notion is the reason why, for many of us, faith simply "doesn't work" as it should. Instead of faith being this type of formulaic procedure, it is designed to be the life and the lifestyle of a believer.

Romans 1:17

"For in it the righteousness of God is revealed from faith to faith; as it is written, "The just shall live by faith."

In Hebrews 11:1 Paul was not giving us a definition of faith, the Bible is not a dictionary. The writer of Hebrews was writing to Jews who were in need of a simplistic approach and understanding of faith. They were married to the law. We are not.

Hebrews 10:38-39

"Now the just shall live by faith; but if anyone draws back, My soul has no pleasure in him. But we are not of those who draw back to perdition, but of those who believe to the saving of the soul."

So, it's important to see the context of which it is used. The faith that Paul was talking about was a faith that doesn't draw back but one that keeps you on the journey. The faith mentioned in Hebrews 11 is a kind of faith that is based on evidence of things the people who needed it never saw. The people of Israel in Moses' day had the serpent as an evidence and type (an emblem of evil on the cross), but they never saw the full picture. They had goats as an evidence of sacrifice, but they never witnessed the real sacrifice taking place.

Hebrews 11:40 & 12:2

"God having provided something better for us, that they should not be made perfect apart from us" with the best they had, they never made perfect...Looking unto Jesus, the author and finisher of our faith, who for the joy that was set before Him endured the cross, despising the shame, and has sat down at the right hand of the throne of God"

Faith is the life and lifestyle of every born-again believer in Jesus Christ. It's not a tool that merely helps us live. It's the directive compass that guides, decides and dictates how we live.

Romans 10:5-9

For Moses writes about the righteousness which is of the law, "The man who does those things shall live by them.

But the righteousness of faith speaks in this way, "Do not say in your heart, 'Who will ascend into heaven?' (that is, to bring Christ down from above) or, "'Who will descend into the abyss?'" (that is, to bring Christ up from the dead). But what does it say? "The word is near you, in your mouth and in your heart (that is, the word of faith which we preach): that if you confess with your mouth the Lord Jesus and believe in your heart that God has raised Him from the dead, you will be saved."

Under the Law (verse 5) it is about what we do (and by that I mean works, performance, acts of labour), but under Grace (verse 6) it's all about grace, faith and our words. Faith abides. Faith endures. Faith perseveres. Faith never gives up. Faith is a knowing, and because Christ is the embodiment of Faith, to know Him is to believe in the power of His finished works. The Message of Christ brings faith.

Paul consistently reminds us that the Law is the letter and it kills so it cannot give you faith, we are born of faith and whatever is born of God overcomes the world. So I agree with a friend of mine (world renowned gospel artist and anointed Minister) Michael

Mahendere when he sings the songs that says, "I am a Victor, I win every battle, in Jesus name I am an overcomer!" Praise God!

Hosea 4:6

My people are cut off (excluded, or are not able to participate) for lack of knowledge.

In this verse, there are two kinds of people that are cut off. On one hand there are those who are cut off simply because: i) they just don't know and there are others who are cut off because: ii) they know the truth but choose not to act upon it. iii) The will of God in your life will not happen in spite of you but it will happen because of you. We should never underestimate the overriding power of human will.

Hebrews 2:1-3

"Therefore we must give the more earnest heed to the things we have heard, lest we drift away. For if the word spoken through angels proved steadfast, and every transgression and disobedience received a just reward, how shall we escape if we neglect so great a salvation,

which at the first began to be spoken by the Lord, and was confirmed to us by those who heard Him"

In conclusion, you have to understand that the will of God in your life will not happen in spite of you but because of you. Your life is secured because Christ has purchased your salvation. His sacrifice of love has given us blood bought rights that cannot be contended with, opposed or denied. The love of the Father has provided a way for us to access peace, love, healing, provision, freedom, long life, prosperity, all because of the Covenant Agreement we have with Him through our High Priest, Mediator and joint-heir Jesus Christ.

You do not have to beg for anything from God, just as Jesus never had to beg for anything. He simply asked, and expected it to be done. You are exactly the same! All you now need to do is learn how to receive whatever you want, from your Father. It is that simple. You do not have to struggle anymore, all you need is faith!

Saints, because of what Christ has already done two thousand years ago, you are seated in heavenly places today, far above every principality and power. You are an ambassador of Jesus Christ, you are a royal priesthood, a holy nation and a soldier in the Army of the Lord.

One of my most trusted leaders once brought up a key point that really shifted my revelation on this subject of blood bought rights. He pointed out the fact that covenants and contracts derive their importance based on two very different things. A contract is a document created to protect its signatories from the <u>suspicion, doubt and mistrust</u> they have towards each other. A covenant, however, is an agreement made by two parties based on the <u>love, fellowship, unity of purpose and trust</u> they have towards one another. Think about it, we are asked to sign contracts to ensure we will keep to our promise or agreement. A handshake is not enough, we are required to sign and in some cases, even put up our possessions as collateral in case we default and terminate the conditions of the contract. Everything here is based on the mistrust from one party to another. A contract protects you from harm. A covenant is completely different. It is based on the love and alignment between two separate parties.

Children of God, your covenant promise is to prosper, thrive and be of good health all the days of your life. Of course, this does not mean you will not have challenges and "light afflictions" but it means Christ has purchased a way out and a solution for every problem you will have encounter in life.

This covenant you have with God is because of the sacrifice of Jesus Christ and it is blood bought. It is certified, verified and cannot be annulled. It is an everlasting covenant. Nothing or no one can take it away from you. All you have to do is tap into the truth of this message, internalise it so that you can practice and participate in it. The most precious blood was shed and sacrificed for you and this means that you have been purchased with a price, washed clean of every stain of sin and seated in heavenly places. From this moment onwards, I want you to walk in the authority and power that is legally yours. Be bold, and now that you know who you are, and Whose you are. Go out and make disciples of all nations, occupy territory and do exploits to the glory of the Father in Heaven.

A BLOOD BOUGHT BLESSING

My aim throughout this book was to show you how your life differs from others because of Whose you are. You are a child of God. You are loved more than you can ever imagine. You are the apple of God's eye. His love for you has been proven already. His love for you is the foundation of everything you now have in Christ. Now you are a force to be reckoned with!

When you pray, things happen. When you prophesy, things change. When you decree and declare anything in the Name of our Lord Jesus Christ, Heaven is commissioned to back you up and make sure that "whatever you bound on earth shall be bound in Heaven and whatever you loose on earth shall be loosed in Heaven". You have the keys of the kingdom in your hand right now and it is your destiny to fulfil the agenda of God here on Earth.

The premise of this new authority is based on the Blood that was shed on the Cross where Jesus died. That Blood is the seal that confirms your exemption from the judgement, punishment and wrath of God. You are a special individual who has Kingdom rights.

As Kingdom Believers, we do not conform to the world and its system. No, we influence it. We are here to bring heaven on earth and that starts by accepting Jesus Christ as your personal Lord & Saviour.

If you have yet to do so, I want to prayerfully lead you into a short prayer. Say this after me:

Father, I thank You for loving me. I thank You for sending Your precious Son Jesus Christ here on Earth to lay down His life for me. He died a death that was shameful, even though He committed no sin. I want to say thank you. And I want to accept Jesus Christ today, as my personal Lord & Saviour. Jesus, I believe that you died, was buried and rose again so that my sins can be forgiven once and for all, and so that I have a place prepared for me in your Heavenly Kingdom. I receive eternal life today and I ask that You write my name in the Lamb's Book of Life. Thank you Jesus. I love you!

Congratulations, you have now joined the family of God. Heaven is having a party right now, all because of the decision you have just made. I pray that your life will never be the same after this day. I release the power of peace, love, wisdom, prosperity and grace over your life from today.

Welcome to a new life.

Welcome to a new level of existence.

Welcome to a world where you now reign and rule, because you know who you are, you know whose you are and if anyone asks, you will not hesitate to raise up your voice and state the power of your blood bought rights in Christ.

KEY SCRIPTURE REFERENCES

All scriptures are taken from the New King James Version

Hosea 4:6

My people are destroyed for lack of knowledge.Because you have rejected knowledge, I also will reject you from being priest for Me; Because you have forgotten the law of your God, I also will forget your children.

2 Peter 1:3

...As His divine power has given to us all things that pertain to life and godliness, through the knowledge of Him who called us by glory and virtue...

Philemon 1:6

that the sharing of your faith may become effective by the acknowledgment of every good thing which is in you in Christ Jesus.

2 Timothy 2:15

Be diligent to present yourself approved to God, a worker who does not need to be ashamed, rightly dividing the word of truth.

John 1:45

Philip found Nathanael and said to him, "We have found Him of whom Moses in the law, and also the prophets, wrote—Jesus of Nazareth, the son of Joseph."

John 16:12-13

"I still have many things to say to you, but you cannot bear them now. However, when He, the Spirit of truth, has come, He will guide you into all truth; for He will not speak on His own authority, but whatever He hears He will speak; and He will tell you things to come.

Hebrews 8:6

But now He has obtained a more excellent ministry, inasmuch as He is also Mediator of a better covenant, which was established on better promises.

Galatians 1:6-7

I marvel that you are turning away so soon from Him who called you in the grace of Christ, to a different gospel, which is not another; but there are some who trouble you and want to pervert the gospel of Christ.

Ephesians 1:18
...the eyes of your understanding being enlightened; that you may know what is the hope of His calling, what are the riches of the glory of His inheritance in the saints...

Acts 20:2
Now when he had gone over that region and encouraged them with many words, he came to Greece...

Hebrews 11:1-2
Now faith is the substance of things hoped for, the evidence of things not seen. For by it the elders obtained a good testimony.

Romans 3:20
Therefore by the deeds of the law no flesh will be justified in His sight, for by the law is the knowledge of sin.

Ephesians 1:15-16

Therefore I also, after I heard of your faith in the Lord Jesus and your love for all the saints, do not cease to give thanks for you, making mention of you in my prayers...

Hebrews 11:40

God having provided something better for us, that they should not be made perfect apart from us.

Romans 8:6-9

For to be carnally minded is death, but to be spiritually minded is life and peace. Because the carnal mind is enmity against God; for it is not subject to the law of God, nor indeed can be. So then, those who are in the flesh cannot please God. But you are not in the flesh but in the Spirit, if indeed the Spirit of God dwells in you. Now if anyone does not have the Spirit of Christ, he is not His.

Ephesians 2:11-12

Therefore remember that you, once Gentiles in the flesh—who are called Uncircumcision by what is called the Circumcision made in the flesh by hands—

that at that time you were without Christ, being aliens from the commonwealth of Israel and strangers from the covenants of promise, having no hope and without God in the world.

Jeremiah 31:31-33
"Behold, the days are coming, says the Lord, when I will make a new covenant with the house of Israel and with the house of Judah—not according to the covenant that I made with their fathers in the day that I took them by the hand to lead them out of the land of Egypt, My covenant which they broke, though I was a husband to them, says the Lord. But this is the covenant that I will make with the house of Israel after those days, says the Lord: I will put My law in their minds, and write it on their hearts; and I will be their God, and they shall be My people.

Hebrews 2:1-3
Therefore we must give the more earnest heed to the things we have heard, lest we drift away. For if the word spoken through angels proved steadfast, and every transgression, sin and disobedience (committed by us) received a just reward, how shall we escape if we

neglect so great a salvation, which at the first began to be spoken by the Lord, and was confirmed to us by those who heard Him.

Romans 10:5-9

For Moses writes about the righteousness which is of the law, "The man who does those things shall live by them." But the righteousness of faith speaks in this way, "Do not say in your heart, 'Who will ascend into heaven?' " (that is, to bring Christ down from above) or, " 'Who will descend into the abyss?' " (that is, to bring Christ up from the dead). But what does it say? "The word is near you, in your mouth and in your heart" (that is, the word of faith which we preach): that if you confess with your mouth the Lord Jesus and believe in your heart that God has raised Him from the dead, you will be saved.

Hebrews 12:2

...looking unto Jesus, the author and finisher of our faith, who for the joy that was set before Him endured the cross, despising the shame, and has sat down at the right hand of the throne of God.

James 1:23-25

For if anyone is a hearer of the word and not a doer, he is like a man observing his natural face in a mirror; for he observes himself, goes away, and immediately forgets what kind of man he was. But he who looks into the perfect law of liberty and continues in it, and is not a forgetful hearer but a doer of the work, this one will be blessed in what he does.

Romans 10:17

So then faith comes by hearing, and hearing by the word of God.

Hebrews 11:3-5

By faith we understand that the worlds were framed by the word of God, so that the things which are seen were not made of things which are visible. By faith Abel offered to God a more excellent sacrifice than Cain, through which he obtained witness that he was righteous, God testifying of his gifts; and through it he being dead still speaks. By faith Enoch was taken away so that he did not see death, "and was not found, because God had taken him"; for before he was taken he had this testimony, that he pleased God.

1 Corinthians 1:18

For the message of the cross is foolishness to those who are perishing, but to us who are being saved it is the power of God. For it is written: "I will destroy the wisdom of the wise, and bring to nothing the understanding of the prudent."

John 6:51

I am the living bread which came down from heaven. If anyone eats of this bread, he will live forever; and the bread that I shall give is My flesh, which I shall give for the life of the world."

Jeremiah 31:31-32

"Behold, the days are coming, says the Lord, when I will make a new covenant with the house of Israel and with the house of Judah— not according to the covenant that I made with their fathers in the day that I took them by the hand to lead them out of the land of Egypt, My covenant which they broke, [a]though I was a husband to them, says the Lord.

Mark 2:22

And no one puts new wine into old wineskins; or else the new wine bursts the wineskins, the wine is spilled, and the wineskins are ruined. But new wine must be put into new wineskins."

1 John 4:19

We love Him because He first loved us.

Hebrews 8:10

For this is the covenant that I will make with the house of Israel after those days, says the Lord: I will put My laws in their mind and write them on their hearts; and I will be their God, and they shall be My people.

Mark 16:17-18

And these signs will follow those who believe: In My name they will cast out demons; they will speak with new tongues; they will take up serpents; and if they drink anything deadly, it will by no means hurt them; they will lay hands on the sick, and they will recover."

Colossians 1:25-27

...of which I became a minister according to the stewardship from God which was given to me for you, to fulfil the word of God, the mystery which has been hidden from ages and from generations, but now has been revealed to His saints. To them God willed to make known what are the riches of the glory of this mystery among the Gentiles: which is Christ in you, the hope of glory.

James 1:25

But he who looks into the perfect law of liberty and continues in it, and is not a forgetful hearer but a doer of the work, this one will be blessed in what he does.

Romans 5:5

Now hope does not disappoint, because the love of God has been poured out in our hearts by the Holy Spirit who was given to us.

Romans 16:25

Now to Him who is able to establish you according to my gospel and the preaching of Jesus Christ, according to the revelation of the mystery kept secret since the world began...

2 Peter 3:16

...as also in all his epistles, speaking in them of these things, in which are some things hard to understand, which untaught and unstable people twist to their own destruction, as they do also the rest of the Scriptures.

Hebrews 8:6

But now He has obtained a more excellent ministry, inasmuch as He is also Mediator of a better covenant, which was established on better promises.

John 5:39

You search the Scriptures, for in them you think you have eternal life; and these are they which testify of Me.

John 20:31

...but these are written that you may believe that Jesus is the Christ, the Son of God, and that believing you may have life in His name.

2 Samuel 9:1-12

Now David said, "Is there still anyone who is left of the house of Saul, that I may show him [a]kindness for Jonathan's sake?" And there was a servant of the house of Saul whose name was Ziba. So when they had called him to David, the king said to him, "Are you Ziba?" He said, "At your service!" Then the king said, "Is there not still someone of the house of Saul, to whom I may show the kindness of God?" And Ziba said to the king, "There is still a son of Jonathan who is lame in his feet." So the king said to him, "Where is he?" And Ziba said to the king, "Indeed he is in the house of Machir the son of Ammiel, in Lo Debar." Then King David sent and brought him out of the house of Machir the son of Ammiel, from Lo Debar. Now when Mephibosheth the son of Jonathan, the son of Saul, had come to David, he fell on his face and prostrated himself. Then David said, "Mephibosheth?" And he answered, "Here is your servant!" So David said to him, "Do not fear, for I will surely show you kindness for Jonathan your father's sake, and will restore to you all the land of Saul your grandfather; and you shall eat bread at my table continually." Then he bowed himself, and said,

"What is your servant, that you should look upon such a dead dog as I?" And the king called to Ziba, Saul's servant, and said to him, "I have given to your master's son all that belonged to Saul and to all his house. You therefore, and your sons and your servants, shall work the land for him, and you shall bring in the harvest, that your master's son may have food to eat. But Mephibosheth your master's son shall eat bread at my table always." Now Ziba had fifteen sons and twenty servants. Then Ziba said to the king, "According to all that my lord the king has commanded his servant, so will your servant do." "As for Mephibosheth," said the king, "he shall eat at my table like one of the king's sons." Mephibosheth had a young son whose name was Micha. And all who dwelt in the house of Ziba were servants of Mephibosheth.

Galatians 1:11-12
But I make known to you, brethren, that the gospel which was preached by me is not according to man. For I neither received it from man, nor was I taught it, but it came through the revelation of Jesus Christ.

RECOMMENDED READING

Bought with Blood: The Divine Exchange at the Cross
Derek Prince

The Blood
Benny Hinn

The Believer's Authority
Kenneth Hagin

King's Cross: Understanding the Life and
Death of the Son of God
Timothy Keller

The Voice of Faith
Cynthia Brazelton

For more information, resources and educational material on the topic of your Blood Bought Rights, go to YourBloodBoughtRights.com today and equip yourself with all the additional teaching material that is available to you.

Printed in Poland
by Amazon Fulfillment
Poland Sp. z o.o., Wrocław